My Son

KM Wegelius

My Po&ry

Collection of Poems

My blog: https://kmwegelius.blogspot.com

Cover : Mikael
Interior: Mikael
Translation: Michaela Schiltz

Publisher: BoD – Books on Demand, Helsinki, Finland
Manufacturer: BoD – Books on Demand, Norderstedt, Germany

ISBN: 978-952-80-6701-6

Contents

I Natural

March

The sun showers intense light,
painting the last snowbanks purple

The first day of March is heated by the logs and their
chemical transformation play

On my writing desk, in a cloudy glass of water, a greenish
pussy willow

In the opposite window of a dilapidated neighboring
house, a young mother appears breastfeeding

The reflection of the window obscures her image,
rejected by the echo of swaying church bells

The downy, yellowish branches of the pussy willow curve
from the glass, like the mosaic of terrene tentacles of
Amos Rex.

A passing lane in the sky, silver strings of clouds make
headway after February, before tired April, one ordinary
March

September came

…and its unfinished clouds,
with themeless drops falling from them,
dripping like a runny nose,

damp stories as remaining leaves cover my house in
empty verses.

Until an epic snowfall takes over,
tragically banishing autumn into obscurity.

October

Everything that smelled of summer withered away

Bright warm colors became deeper before the end

My friends crouch into their caves like the bear retreats
into hibernation

Silence has thrown its purple quilt over the sunset

Behind my window, darkness plays hide and seek with
my reading lamp

I am writing a poem in key minor, about living hope.

From cold to warm

From the North Sea wind
frigid, a tear wells from intensity,
drowning into the waves of the tumultuous sea
and mixing with the surf,

suddenly finds a way to your skin,
in a most beautiful and warm moment

Sunflower

Like a downpour, the moments of my life fall around me in drops, running into most as I walk quickly, and getting drenched when I stand still, I understand the rain better.

Should I run to find shelter from the rain or should I jump from puddle to puddle?

Rain soaks the seeds waiting underground, encouraging them to grow, erupting with sunflower rays.

Poplar

The last leaf of a poplar tree falls
in the darkness of the night,
there is a beauty hidden from view
going down amongst the others

and composes

Leaf in the wind

Was this what I was waiting for,
one more leaf left
The flutter in the wind tells of autumn's arrival

Delivers that which is most beautiful in itself
In colors the hope, in forms the joy, in movement the
belief

The coming spring's new colors
another chance they give

Micro or macro

Is our sun a spark from the Big Bang

the spark that glowed for billions of years,
 so immense and important to us

Is a spark from our campfire someone else's sun
going out in seconds for us,
and for others lasting billions of ages

Blind Cat

A blind cat always looks straight ahead

A blind cat sees sound in 9D

A blind cat knows who you are even if you stray

A blind cat sees the most beautiful world

Cabin shore

The water on the shore is too cloudy to reveal its mud bottom.

The windows of my cabin show pictures of willows on the water's edge.

 Pigeons coo late into the evening, as the sun sets,

A few passers-by stop to sit on the gut stones,

In the light of this yard there is no tomorrow,

I see the days through my window,

Staring at shoreless plains.

Release

My smile repeats already every day, my mind is lighter than the butterflies in the sky

Relaxing all day long, forgetting the physical labor I so needed

Intelligence brings the simplicity of understanding

The wind transports mindless clouds to the shore of the sky

The sea eagle bows under the protection of its nesting tree

The grass snake disappears into a hole in the rocks

I am among them the wild apple tree

The drawn out fall on my island turns towards night's cold embrace

Islet

Rainwater that has flowed into the crevices of the bedrock
quickly evaporates by the sun

The boathouse paint has faded into gray
Fishing nets have dried in and burned out by sun
The autumn breeze ebbs and flows on the shoreline

In the middle of the islet,
a man leaning on the bend of the only pine tree,
surrounded by nature,
nearly sixty years old.

II The last of humankind

The sun is on the verge of death, humans have evolved for billions of years. The last solitary man waits for the last sunrise. How have we survived for so long, what lonely thoughts are there as the end grows near, what comes after the end.

- I am alert and focused. I want to
perform as is required by my abilities.
I come to my solutions based on my
experiences and training.
I don't let fear or paralysis take up
space in my mind.

We did not find intelligent life or a
suitable place to live on another planet.
Neither could be found. But we succeeded
here. We had a long, even fortunate streak
of adaptation.

- I survived this long, too long, alone.
I should feel something, the feelings
disappear into obscurity amidst complete
loneliness, no mutual joys or sorrows to
share.

No new members of the species have been born for 269 years. The last to be born did not adapt to the most significant changes that took place on the sun. There were only a few left over from the previous period.

- My only memory of the past is a picture of a man wearing a spacesuit on the surface of the moon. The horizon reveals a beautiful blue planet. Can it be this same, gray Earth.

A mutation in my immune system has allowed me to be the lone survivor. In my youth, I wanted to serve humanity and lead us toward a better future.

54 years have passed since the death of other humans. They were brutally attacked by an insidious virus.

- Of course I am afraid, I'm not trying to hide that, I will vigilantly perform my duties until the end. My job is to find a way out of solar system which advances toward it's end.

- Did I fail when I couldn't find what I was looking for. I did my job well. Limited resources did not support my efforts. Fortunately, the solution was all around us. In time, we came to understand that.

The gravitational pull of the sun and the effects of radiation prevented contact with other organic states of consciousness. They always existed. Not in space but right next to us.

We managed to get to the moon, such a short distance of the required journey. Like a small jump, even though we needed infinite light years.

- Why do I keep trying? I am so lonely,
I want to find someone or an answer.
Are we the only ones after all.

After finding a solution nearby, we
adapted to everything. Carbon dioxide
fluctuations, meteor attacks, recurring
ice ages and their subsequent floods, the
Earth was actually ruled by bacteria.
Someone, somewhere always survived and
transformed. The only ones left now are me
and my tired sun.

We did not drift into the material
scarcity of dystopia, we made a choice to
shift from the physical to the mental, and
we progressed to a whole new level. We
achieved the beauty of intangibility.

Our physical state diminished to near
obscurity. Our development focused on our
brain's ability to examine and process an
extensive amount of information.

Our population declined as evolution progressed. Physicality, the ability to move and function became unnecessary. Intelligence, understanding, and the ability to learn grew in strength. Only the intelligent survived and were able to reproduce.

The graying of millions of years of clouds blurred visibility to other worlds, the moon, the sun, and the stars.

- Shall I close my eyes or look straight at my destruction. I don't want to forfeit the last, enchanting sight.

The amount of oxygen in the atmosphere decreased significantly, for which the number of red blood cells compensated. We finally got an increase in oxygen when the fossil period ended. It was the beginning of millions of years of ecological resuscitation.

- The shadow drawn by the hand of my sundial fades with each rotation. All that remains are bursts and flashes on the orange surface. They lack power and effectiveness.

Before it expires, the sun looks friendly as the color becomes warmer.

- I know that when the final explosion comes, the atmosphere will burn so fast that I won't have time to feel the end.

- Dare I feel happy with all the evil that has occurred on this planet. Happy I couldn't find new planets to export all of our madness.

Within the final explosion is beauty and raging violence, a terrible amount of agony is targeted specifically at me.

Large expanding red pearl. The last test of strength followed by an explosive collapse. The masses of our solar system merge into a large destructive asteroid.

- Like a catapult, we launch toward other galaxies, carrying our dust wherever it goes. We move to new planets, where the task will be fulfilled.

Maybe again, after billions of years, something new will ripen from our dust.

- The first disturbance of the morning
sun, past the roundness of the earth makes
me hopeful.

We solved the problem of overpopulation
and lack of nutrition, sufficient, clean
water became the hardest nut to crack.
Indeed, the formula is simple H + 2 + O =
water. Yet so problematic. We overcame the
critical point. Marine biologist Greta's
thesis created water and coolness.

Loneliness is the heaviest, without
knowing, we bought a ticket to loneliness
with our glorification of technology,
video games, and enhanced reality.

- I would like to have met the one who
made me one more time, my mother.

In the folds of time, we made contacts
with other generations and time periods,
the encounters were illogical

I saw myself as a child or very old,
beyond this day, my last.

- When a person ceases to exist, the earth
disappears, the sun explodes and burns
out, how it all feels to me.

No artificial intelligence beyond human capability can replace a stupid person next to you.

Everything changed when we figured out how to pass gravity.

When life lasts for hundreds of years, the desire to hurry disappears, as the end approaches for external reasons, it intensifies.

Science and scientists found solutions as we focused on the essential security of life. With funds released from the war budget, we corrected many injustices.

We have survived with genuine encounters with obstacles and found solutions, our ability to change is limitless.

There is no solution for this, the cruelty of the universe does not offer mercy, this is final.

- I would like to believe that reason won, but we lost something important, the ability to love one another.

There's an old saying about life in a bubble, a negative idea of a limited paradigm. Afterwards all life could only be possible in a bubble. Neurotic plastic bubble poppers became even more neurotic survivors within the plastic bubble.

Faith in the future is impossible for
those who have not experienced a miracle.

Synthetic water, synthetic bread, millions
of years, natural is not even a memory. My
synthetic heart beats less than 10 times
per minute, I steadily breathe ventilator
air.

After each day a new day rises… children
walk the paths paved by their parents…
after today the indentation of these paths
disappear, there will be no new
footprints.

Billions of other suns could have been
found with life-sustaining planets
orbiting them.

Every memory is built on our emotions. We remember our emotions, not the details of events. Only our feelings can be true.

Already for a long time there has been orange everywhere, bright orange light reflecting through a cloud of dust.

We could have continued to despise one another, fear one another, and destroy one another. Instead, we decided to develop together, learn together and survive together.

- The last flash, like God's angry lightning striking upon me. Could I be forgiven, receive grace or damnation, will I finally be free.

Multinational corporations, super power
countries and different religions' desire
for greatness, power and control over
others was a massive obstacle to learning
a new, harmonious and more peaceful order
to life. The capacity for making a new
kind of contact introduced solutions to
replace dysfunctional systems.

- Where are my mother, my children, my
family in my moment of distress. The
organic machine has taken care of me for
too long. When the last explosion comes, I
won't feel fear, bitterness, or anger.
I do not feel. Could this be a relief that
brings purpose to the sustained tragedy.

The development of solar wind sails was
canceled, concentrating instead on the
ability of our own planet to tolerate the
homo sapien species. This created space
for the idea of us rather than me. With
collective learning came our experience of
remembering the future.

Nobler, wiser levels of understanding and being were found. They were not spatial, scientific, or mathematical formulas. We found the lost lobes of our own brain activity, experiencing unity after the fallen barriers of unlimited omnipotence.

Our resilience against viruses and bacteria was fixed with genetic alteration and chronological time manipulation.

- I remember the moments between the beginning and the end. By the end, I mean memories of our species and solar system disappeared. We continue our endless journey into infinity as space dust.

Those who knew had to struggle through adjustment periods. The physicist's ability to transition to weightlessness was more difficult than that of a linguist. And vice versa as our communication moved from the web to our consciousness.

The multidimensionality of consciousness and the momentary continuum of smoke-like transforming entities created new levels for our understanding.

The perception of two-way memory, the understanding of three-dimensional time, and the disappearance of one-dimensional gravity revealed the complexity of a new consciousness.

Thought accesses time, memory shifts, there is no place for them. The unstoppable flow of thoughts is like a circular palindrome in our multi-dimensional subconscious.

- I know what will happen, I will welcome it all with joy, expelling the burden of my cold loneliness.

Did we reach our highest level, could we have created even more potential. Why. We are being destroyed by the insensitive force of nature in space. Why not earlier.

- Because I'm alone, no one can give me a Turing test. I would like to know if I am actually a human or a machine with a conscious.

The ability to communicate is in us as soon as we are born. We learn the language and its structures as we grow. But, even without words, the ability is already clear in our body language and in our facial expressions.

- Power outages have repeatedly complicated my research. A series of solar storms persist before the final calm.

The development of superhuman artificial intelligence quickly led to an incomprehensible unlimited singularity for man.

The insignificance of humanity drove us to the brink of extinction. Our limitations are what came to our rescue and allowed for our preservation. We could not have reached our limitations without being destroyed and returned to the essentials with the help of new technologies.

- If the infinity of billions of galaxies
that seems boundless, is just an empty
void of consciousness after me, then why?

What is the purpose of everything? Why
didn't anyone come to this "Dim Blue Dot"?
Our heavenly dreams did not come true.
Behind the dust fog there was no savior.

At some point, in the wasteland between
science and emotion, we lost our sense of
direction. Especially now in my eternal
loneliness, it has been difficult to
understand the purpose of the events. It
is difficult to be all alone. I wish I
could share these moments with someone.

Life in space is impossible

- I enjoy the silence in my loneliness, no matter how much I hate this silence. It's scary to be solely responsible for everything. I have learned to let go in order to survive.

- I will die today, of course, everybody dies, it feels inconsolable to know and wait, scared. No one to mourn, no one to offer forgiveness of sins or to pray for me. Would I pray for myself, I never learned if it would help.

- If there were a way to survive. I could turn off all systems, be quiet, close my eyes. Disengage from self-awareness. No one injures me or insults me, I am safe. Uncertain only in the face of the terrible destructive power of nature.

- Do I hear my mother say 'We have to keep getting up after every fall, we have to continue to move forward after every set-back'.

- I would like to believe that the future exists, clean air that can be breathed, other people whose touch can be felt.

In order to die, one must first be alive,
one must have a human paradigm,
not souls in terabits, developed by
algorithms and stored in memory gels.

- A flash, like a muscle spasm in the
corner of my eye

- I am aware of my soul, even after the
total destruction. The universe is not an
endless emptiness. I'll find out what it
is.

III Imaginative

Stories have always been told

There things happen that can't in real life

Mysteries transport to far away places

Usually wanting that escape

Shangri-La

I found a good place,
I got lost in the garden of beauty
I heard silence,
I was welcomed
I felt other people's feelings also,
I noticed a communal strength,
I saw the horizon and the purpose,
I sensed a wordless acceptance

there, in that moment, I lived my whole life,
could I stay?
did I even exist anymore?

everything, everything changed again

Sauna elf

I have seen the sauna elf peeking out from under the floorboards.

The other night I surprised him while he was dozing, with the emanating off of the sauna stones.
I would have liked him to answer a few of my interesting questions.
Does he live as a hermit only in this sauna?
Has he met the elf from the smoke sauna on the neighboring island?
Is it he who sings to the tune of Kalevala on autumn evenings, among the birch whisks in the cooling sauna?
If he ever wants to go to the market, does he change into his Sunday best, or does he remain in his regular elf clothes?
Does he walk in the middle of the road winking and greeting the daughters of the neighborhood?
Does he kick his shoes off and go dancing in jazz clubs in order to meet female elves?
Can an elf fall in love like a human can?
Can a sauna elf move away from his sauna forever?
Does an elf look at his watch, it's already late, he has to go back.

Hansha's laptop

My operating system would like to live forever,
but the quarterly economy and owner control won't
stand still.

I would like to meet a floppy disk from the early DOS
days, but their FAT is no longer supported

Along the strand of days, memory capacities are
inevitably passed from year to year, generations of
processors follow one another

Where today I write in the cloud,
there was a time when I would fiddle back and forth with
my pen

Longing for peace

Longing for peace is a high mountain
Peace is only on top of that mountain
which humans have not conquered
Peace comes without having to try

I equip myself for peace

On the side of the Northern watchtower,

I cannot imagine anyone would attack from there,

with its endless sea spray and ice daggers flying in the air,

I turn my attention to the border fire in the East,

I wait for the wolves to attack,

Darkness does not distinguish between demons and shadows,

From sleeplessness grows fear,

I believe my crafty adversary approaches from the open plains of the South,

I control the direction on a wall standing higher than evil intentions,

The scout I dispatched to the West sends every signal of the horrors to come,

Amidst all of the threats I feel calmness settle in,

I fight for my peace.

The path of life

Shiny and intact, completely empty inside

A few obvious scratches on the surface,
knows everything, imagining so

Severe wounds lie under the surface, others with more
significance takes your time, but gives back so much

The Shell worn-out ,
bag of Thoughts, heavy as a wet cloak

Dump it all into a cart,
and quietly cross over the bridge

The life cycle of dreams

The anatomy of dreams like a soldier's helmet
Bruised in battles
full of holes after the war has ended

Golem

In the late evening I watch the fading light. After dark, I
hear moaning, rustling, chirping, screaming all around
me
Listening to them, the night is eternal
In the darkest hours of the morning, the sounds
grow louder still, surrounding the sides of my bed,
ensuring that sleep does not conquer anxiety.
The first sliver of morning light chases the evil sounds far
into the corners of the room
leaving a hollow silence that will not be tamed by rest
Emptiness rings in my ears preying on the mind with a
new struggle
Exhausted, I am rescued by the voices of my neighbor's
radio and rustling of keys in the stairwell.
A moped starts up on the same side of the street that the
janitor and mailman are chatting on
I finally open the curtains to reveal dark clouds gathering
in the eastern sky

A Woman's strength

In a forgotten town, on a nameless street,
in an unnumbered house, behind a door,
without a doorbell,
under the front stairway,
stashed in a windowless closet, lived a Woman.

A woman whose dreams glowed and glittered,
and where beauty lived

A woman whose dreams were torn to shreds by the claws
of evil tigers
Tigers, selfish and cruel, cocky and arrogant,
destroying everything intimate and sensitive

Overcoming all obstacles and deceiving those they
cannot, passing everything frightening,
defying their own demons, exceeding their own strength,
tearing their way to their own refuge

In her loneliness, in her own closet, slowly, the Woman
collects the fragments of herself, becoming stronger,
growing whole again, becoming the heroine, facing her
tigers.

The Woman rises past the former
Woman so beautiful, with such endurance

Behind her, others follow.

Bar ghost

A man sat next to me at the bar and told me all of his darkest secrets, his deepest feelings, his thoughts about life, everything that made him a person.

Captivated, I immersed myself in his story.

When he left, I didn't know how to reach him,
I didn't ask for his name, number, address.

I think of him often, although I don't remember his philosophies or beliefs

I remember his bowed step,
the figure that disappeared through the bar door

What you left behind is not important,
only what we could have been if you had stayed.

Mom

With mom is home,

There is no need to perform,

to be somebody else,

to say how things are,

what we agree, I do,

so good,

always

For dad

The moon guides dad rowing on the lake.

I observe the movements of the boat from the foggy beach of Härmälä.

Would I make the same decisions and movements?

My own moon, guide me

Closest to me

When I understand the limitless in the dark of the night,
my thoughts drift towards you, Mother

When I recognize the core wisdom contained in humility
I bow to my Father

When the shadows of my travel companion disappear
next to me
I know that my Sister's torch will lead me back to my
path home

When the ruby rays of my sun fade
I believe my Son will ignite a new spark

Moon threat

Waking up to a commotion outside
people shouted incomprehensibly to one another
Car horns blaring, everyone scrambling

In the sky, the moon moved noticeably quickly
it was bigger than ever before
Falling behind the trees

Unable to gather my thoughts
behind the bend and the rooftops of the city,
the moon appears quickly
now bigger, even faster

Just a moment to think about how to act,
where to go, with whom,

new rotation, now the moon is so close it is audible
I see the craters, I feel the gravitation,
I could reach out and touch,

Unbelievable paralysis,
the silhouette of life burns into my retinas,

Emptiness

My philosophy on life, the new world order

Hit with an idea, life would be much simpler,
as long as I acted according to the principles
I had decided on beforehand.
I studied life management guides,
which made me feel stuck.
There is too much of everything. Okay. Choose one.
But which?
We are advised to reduce the number of items to one-
hundred.
We are encouraged to take care of our loved ones and
nature.
The third emphasizes the importance of economic
management.

A brilliant thought popped into my mind.
I will create my own life order.
It will finally provide answers to everything.
Not an easy task, this requires a lot of thought and
reflection.

Along with others, you should belong to different groups.
Family, relatives, colleagues, support groups, religion,
political party, nation, clan, team
there must be **TRUST** between them
groups should merge with other groups when they meet
on common ground

When everyone belongs to everyone else's communities
through the combination of their own groups,
there will be no more conflict,
Fantastic.

The most important creative power , **LOVE**,
 giving and receiving,
providing and accepting
to bring hope and longing,
spreading it to a lucky companion,
the deepest meaning of life,
The object of all, near and far,
Maintain love as your outer shell
Hide your anger, bury it in the deepest abyss,
Lovely.

I was overjoyed when I realized who I was,
I accumulated many trials throughout the journey
I was able to move past them,
Prior to that I only dared to be afraid
Now **I DARE** to be me,
Along the way I hated the unknown,
when I began to recognize myself,
my anger subsided
I also dared to face the surreal,
The Joy of Expanding Consciousness

We are frozen in what surrounds our bodies
within the smoke of customs and habits
smoke does not limit our movements by disabling our
vision preventing action from moving within
TOUCHING distance of one another, punch holes for
ventilation and burst through the walls and ceilings to see
everyone whose touch I'm waiting for, everyone whose
touch I was groping for in the middle of the smoke,
Nice.

Be seen by another, as if nothing has happened,
An **EMOTIONAL** bubble inside me with the power of a
volcanic eruption, I let it out, for all to see
the incendiary force defines me, shows others who I am
I, myself, must be called, cleansing of true emotion
growing a garden of beauty around myself
Take care of your garden, you get nourishment from it,
Refreshing.

Empathy can't be taught, or can it? Why hasn't evolution
prioritized the most empathetic?
Only the toughest and most selfish are the survivors,
Now we have survived as winners against nature
It is the turn of an era of intellect
The next stage of evolution cultivates **CARING**,
Those who are able to take care of themselves and others
provide a chance for a new kind of survival,
We defeat ourselves, the evil within us,
the Savior,

You. I give you my most valuable possession,
to be kept in your immaterial briefcase's secret chamber,
When you feel the weight of this show of trust on your
metaphorical shoulders, you realize how much
I **APPRECIATE**,
When I show appreciation towards you,
 I get back double the appreciation from you,
Moving

No one should be **AFRAID** to say $2 + 2 = 4$
No one should be forced to understand that the answer is
in fact, 5, or in some cases, 3,
By chance it could be all three if the bigger one wants it,
Winces

That's all,
My whole philosophy of life
I have decided to **love** you,
I **trust** you completely,
I **dare** to **touch** you and
I feel **respect** for you.
I **care** about you and everyone else,
and I take away my **fear** of everyone else because
I **trust** them to do the same.
It's that simple.
Now I can continue,
life and the world are in order.

IV The phases of love

IV.I Creating love

For you

Didn't I miss your closeness,
even though I came to you in silence

Didn't I think you'd fill the dark places with your light

Hope and fear had we both
The desire to give only to you
made you mine

Seeker

I'm trying to find a way to your soul,
I'm walking inside your body wearing blue,
disposable slippers,

I reach higher, beyond your chest
I see the lights of the galaxy twinkling,

the constellations change places faster than my
comprehension can withstand, at a speed that
clouds my perception,
wings of plastic wrap grow from my arms,
leaping into a free fall,
my wings lift me higher and higher,
infinite space inside you,
I, a shoreless explorer,
I search for your dreams, your secret thoughts,
evidence that you care and love,

When you suddenly open your eyes,
I see down the corridor revealing the way to your soul,

the opportunity to see everything as you do,
through you,
you love

Do I doubt it ?

Did I hear you right, Did you call out to me?

Did I hear in your voice, the secret of your longing?

Did somebody else hear you speak?

Did I hear my inner voice doubting, hesitating?

Did I actually hear myself saying "How can I live without you anymore?"

Did I actually hear wrong?

Our timeless love

I admired your joy for a whole day,

I watched your beauty for two nights

For three months I learned your secrets,

For four years I exposed your modesty

For five springs I observed the growth of your blossoms,

I would like to share six hundred years with you,

For an eternity your skin glows in whale songs,

Just a moment by your side,

That moment, all the times within

The ego of my senses

Can I believe my eyes when your beauty approaches

Can I believe my ears when your words say you want to stay

Can I believe the skin of my hands when, with your permission, I let my fingers drown in your

hair

Do I believe my sense of smell when I detect the inviting scent of readiness on you

Can I believe the flavors hot on my tongue as our lips meet in an insatiable kiss

Do my senses lie to me when my lust extinguishes all reason

Calmly, age allows me to understand as such,

in youth, the lie of my senses could carry me away

I'm writing this now so I can connect these times,

time doesn't give in to my thoughts,

though I feel for the first time

Like a movie

Your kisses didn't feel exactly the way they should feel

Even a bad experience is better than no experience at all

If you were music, I'd want to live from song to song in
an endless music video

Nothing really exists, everything is all the time, either
coming or going

I guess I'm not who I think I am or who you think you
love

You do what you want, it's good, you create boundaries
which have to be broken, it's a beautiful and difficult life
with you and without compromise, together,
when free, love never disappears

For the first time I felt and loved, so I knew
I wanted it to last forever, it's only a moment,
The beauty of your love turns me into an ugly scumbag,
a crying imbecile

I'm shy and timid, intimidated by your physicality

I asked you to be my wife, Your answer was simply 'No',
you left me wanting even more

I lived with you, like a dream, I strove for honesty, purity
and freedom, I didn't know how I always wanted the
truth, I think it might hurt

You have to know how to be a good liar in order to be
loved, I don't know anything, you've got it in the bag,

You got that dream job and you're leaving,
I can't let it affect me, nor I it, because you are happy

Have I misunderstood love, it's possible to get the wrong
idea from song lyrics

I would love it if you just asked once in a while,
 You never ask, I hit rock bottom after you leave
like seaweed that settles at the bottom of the sea, I am not
supposed to see the light

I don't deserve it, Everything changes when suspicions
arise,
Did you sleep with him? Many times? How did you do it?
I want you now because you confessed,
We are beasts, we satiate our drive, we waste our love,
will we be forgiven?
The chance we took and lost freed us from ourselves,
Why was I afraid to be set free from love,

Now I am a prisoner in my loneliness, I am either in the
light or in the shadow, looking for companionship

Life would be monotonous if there were only good
moments, a deep connection between us, like the soul of a
wild horse,
I have to find a way out of you, back to where I was
before,

I have to give up in order to achieve something new,
A protective fence has to be built around it,
creating a connection becomes difficult, that's why you
should love everyone who agrees to it,

Do I have disappointment or love inside of me? A love
story should be written more slowly,
There has to be a rhythm, all old wounds should be able
to be healed with words

I'm starting over, getting back together wasn't paradise,
I only knew how to love you
After all we've been through
I want a simple life

IV.II Let's make love

The aftermath

The sounds of our frantic moment quiet down,
our bodies separate, our thoughts intertwine

The memories of yesterday's rain and the colors of this
morning's sunshine mix together in our imaginations
like watercolors in a glass jar

Silently we row the jar's waves,
each stroke of the oar stirring the kaleidoscope of colors in
our thoughts

We can't reach the edges of the jar,
the scenery around us changes,
as if we're floating on the shoreless,
unbroken tantras of love

I don't dare, and I don't want to move,
This moment, here, now,
Always

Your secret cabin

From the lakeshore, I'm starting towards your place
A gentle path begins from the hiding place between rocks
and junipers
In a field surrounded by tall trees,
I see your secret cabin.

From the porch you play the music of life on your violin,
which ignites mixed incense in my mind

I would like to know what you would say if I asked you
"I love you"

Would you answer "The summer-moistened, hot path
needs to be cleared"

Your name

How could I name you?
Not with any meaningful words

More abstract would be more accurate,
words don't describe you at all

As you walk around in your lacy outfits,
the alluring rustle of them rubbing,
that sound is your name

Oh, how even hearing your name awakens my desires

Crazy about love

For so many years I lived the life of a man whom I didn't recognize

I didn't grab ahold of life, I didn't put the pieces together, like my father before me

I went through my youth like a stranger, my marriage, my work, I wandered behind the scenes, without feelings

Shards and fragments under my bare feet,
shards that fell loose from me, what went wrong?

My soul thought it could fly, even though it didn't have wings, it wanted to reach the sky, even though it didn't know how cope on earth

My shell was supposed to break apart and cause pain and suffering, it gave me the ability to fly

What do I want? How do I face myself? How do I start?

I had a dream about the northern lights descending upon the earth, they showed me the direction

The wrath of change, strong, like the death of a twin brother, only me alive

Bubbling when creation begins, a sense of redemption, clinging furiously to its justification

Stumbling, albeit in the right direction,
My life didn't happen anymore
I directed, edited, acted,

Life is a swamp hidden in the middle of the forest
One must struggle thru it

sweaty, bloody, tired, bitten by insects, defiled, naked

I'm winning as long as I feel like I can start over

Dreams are beautiful, you can succeed in dreams,
you can't be satisfied in dreams

From memory I dig up my childhood, I hear its call,
 I remember the whisper, I take it as my guide

On my crusade, I find my youth amidst the darkness
Because eternity do not exist, I pack up what is needed

Sometimes I think others are more confused than me

IV.II Let's be together

Together

Give me a moment of your time,
I promise I won't waste it on futility,

I'll carry it with me from darkness to light,

I'll let my thoughts drift to your shore,
arriving at you like home

Surrender to change

My dear, the leftovers from your cooking and empty
packaging fill our kitchen counters. Apple
cores are blocking the drain.

The quality of your television programming becomes
even more lame.Those who act their life, needy for love
and attention-sick, the fast track of reality tv scripts.

 In the aisles of the grocery store, our carts follow familiar
tracks. Your robotic hands reach for only familiar
products with digital precision.

I miss the adventurer who plundered garden gnomes
from yards to release them on the roof of the bus stop.

At times, I catch a glimpse of my own profile in the
reflection of the display window. I, myself, am no longer
the champion of love who devoted himself to the target,
forgetting everything else.

Cleaning together was a fight scene in our everyday
superhero story. Hand-in- hand in front of the television.
The current runner-up was the comfortable waiting phase
of our ongoing adventure.

There were other sounds under our blankets,
not just desolate sighs when turning slowly from side to
side.

Nothing around us has changed. We want to watch our
own programs on different televisions. That's how well
we remember one another.

Fireguard

Every sunset holds the promise of seeing you again the
next morning

After we first met, I would have given my life to have you

Already the second time I wished for eternal life together

My heart has been on fire at night like a fireguard,
making sure of us all the vanishing happiness

Otherness

Our boundless relationship limits my soul's joy

Our irregular sexuality only flies your kite,
I'm left aimless
only the runner at the other end of the string

Your kite flies in more colorful patterns than you can
imagine

Ditches and rivers make my run a joyless trudge as I try
to support you

This freedom is my prison

In '18

January, our united slow waltz over the floorboards

February, our long passionate kiss on the riverbank.

March, the lingering touch of our sides in front of
Schjerfbeck's self-portrait

April, our galloping trip horseback riding in the Lemdal
grove

May, whispering in French in the dimness of the cinema

June, slips into the bottom of the boat while we relax
among the sails

July, like a warm wind whisping the curls of your bangs

August, rhythms pulse through wine glasses in the jazz
club cellar vault

September is warmed by the eucalyptus sauna of the Koli
spa

October, our passionate embrace in the ladies room of the
cosmic cartoon bar

November, when I can't talk to you, I can only miss you

December, I don't doubt that we won't meet again,
I'll make sure I don't lose you
and these memories of ours

Mom

Her eyes look only so close where the child is

She longs to be somebody else in her own mind,
there is no need to go beyond the backyard gate

The sunny beach of the subconscious is in the land of
tomorrow
From the other room
the rush of emptiness comes immediately
part of me is missing

Pictures do not replace the smell of hair or backs of hands
The memories are just a slight blur of a moment that bears
everything, and that's enough

With her closeness, distances are removed,
without looking for it, it is found

After a while, at the right moment releasing grip,
providing independence

Wedding photographer

The bride glides down the aisle in her white tulle dress
The wedding couple smiles under the rice rain in the sun

The ship bringing wedding guests is too big for this pier

The tense look of the groom in a slow waltz

The wedding couple cuts the cake,
a piece ends up standing upright on a plate

Kisses after every momentary separation

The groom's friends rob the bride
with nylon stockings on her head

The mother-in-law's new husband tests his charm on the
bride's unmarried sister

Let's raise a toast to life and love

A poetic, artistically inclined uncle teaches the party
crowd steps to a jazz beat

The godmother's daughter plays an old love song on the
guitar

To groom as a gift for morning after wedding night,
an artistic boudoir photo of the bride's naked silhouette

Next to the wedding bed, the bride asks for a moment of
her own peace
Is the bride happy after all?

IV.IV Breaking up

Onto the better side

When none of my words interest you anymore

When I've made the mistake
that drains the rest of your cup

When the number of my apologies
can no longer be considered reasonable

When the final collapse happened at night,
I was not present

That's when you escaped my invisible matter
You escaped to the better side of the butterfly curtain

Silent scream

When I lost my loved ones,
where did I belong anymore?

Who would still listen
who could hear so deep inside that they would care

Who would look as if to respect me

Who would I be quiet with, without bothering

It makes me want to scream to be seen

Even without a voice, I am

Just the truth

You tell me with your gestures
that are quieter than silence
The border of autumn has been crossed

The white blanket of winter
hides the path that existed between us

The elusive new spring will not return
The warm winds bring no lighter clouds

My wild cry, across our deep chasm
Your truth is yours
I'll settle for just the truth

Seventh moon

I can already see the seventh full moon from the skylight of my bedroom

Already the seventh since your departing steps left their last traces on my porch

Already seven hundred times I have told the new moon all the layers of my feelings

I couldn't do it for you even once

After the rain

I return to my hometown when the frost is already
stirring in the undergrowth

With my heavy shoes I crush the swaying shadows of the
lilacs

We live in what used to be such a nice little house

On my trip I misspend everything we collected together

I will no longer see a flower in front of me when you
welcome me home

The thorns of the rose I brought will tear the wounds in
your hands

Every rain that falls in our garden carries a threat that
chills my heart

If you turn into me and go away

IV.V Alone and quietly

Anonymous 1

After you, only a sigh separates me
from the thousands of expressions of loneliness

Like a window to my soul
that opens only for the lights to go out again

The mundaneness of feeling returns

Nauvo archipelago

As a child, I put my hand out over the side of our
motorboat as it sped through the water,
the bottom pounding against the waves with every hit of
the wave, a salty crunch stung my hand.

As a child, that is when I realized this forbidden game,
this hot summer damp, feeling of danger,
like playing love with a woman

One winter morning,
while walking on the ice of the same sea bay,
I felt the mercilessness of the freezing wind on my hand,

Love, so many times, love has thrown its stingers at me
I cry when I remember the warmth of my youth,
I imagine it in my old age

Alone again

Only this dry sack under the blanket

The deceptive softness of silk sheets against this rough surface

Dozens of eyes look at me from the windows

Sunrises, disappointing and embittered, observe the clothes of my solitude

Without seeing me

Insufficient

I am a mute singer on the stage of a auditorium,
I am a spaceless astronaut in the cockpit of my tin rocket
I am a kinked IV line in the intensive care unit of a
hospital,
I am a thoughtless poet in the corner of a library,
I am a color-blind painter in front of an empty, white
canvas,
I am an unarmed soldier in an empty trench,
I am an impotent tourist in the backstreets of Amsterdam
I am a fisherman without a net on the open side of the
lake,
You would have been the fulfillment of my dreams
If I had been even something
 or someone else

One hundred loves, one poem

I
loved
many
times
vainly
The temples
silver
strands
tell of
loneliness
In
the dawning
dream
of the long
dark
night
I seek
I long
for
my
love

Cafe Art

I sit in this cafe every night
I've been coming here for years
I'm waiting to meet you here,
whom I don't know yet

I recognized you as soon as you walked in
your beautiful smile, our eyes met

I didn't know how to get up from my table,
I stayed

You enjoyed your coffee,
stepped out,
next time I'll get closer

My loneliness

My loneliness has grown old
bleached in its own black spaces
disintegrated from the inside and dried up on the surface

As I grow older
I distinguish only the strongest contrasts between dark
and light

Dead tired, I leave this old acquaintance
my solitude
and live a little bit

Days of my life

How many days in my life have I been really satisfied
with my body, my mind, my actions, my choices, the
places where I have lived and worked

How many days have I gone in my own direction without
others leading the way

How often have I stayed calm in my body and soul, have
I even wanted that

Do I let the autumn winds knock down thick trunks in
my path,

Do I let the sea monsters frolic on the beach of my bay,

Do I let the storm put out the crackling fire under my
kettle

After I close my eyes everything can prevail,
I open them again,

All my days I live, just on the last I die

Protectionism

I took over a small, abandoned house as my own space

So small, the thin transparency, I covered with curtains,
I hid the innermost layers, the most valuable I preserve
for myself

Behind the curtains I hung misleading camouflage nets
I protect my important, delicate glassy thoughts,
 my worn wooden items
I peek through the cracks in my fabrics at those who are
close to me
scattered human individuals pass by the edges of my
cloud castle without showing even the slightest interest